MY CASE AGAINST RELIGIOUS DOGMA

CHALLENGE YOUR FAITH BY READING THIS BOOK!

SHUBH SRIVASTAVA

ISBN 979-888569658-6

When I was exploring the pondering questions on religion and God, I came to realize that I was surrounded by hard-core believers. Almost all my family members believe in the divine, and I dare to differ. So, I wrote this mini-book for them to understand the process of atheism and skepticism.

Hence, this book is dedicated to my dear-family, especially my father.

Contents

Preface

"**Asking questions is not a crime but not asking questions is!**"

For millennia man has prayed to numerous objects and regarded them as Gods or Goddesses. But in this scientific age, we don't need God to explain natural phenomena. We use the scientific method to perceive the world in which we live.

Greetings everyone! I am a teenage boy from India. My country is the birthplace of many religions like Hinduism, Buddhism, Jainism, and Sikhism. That's why India is also known as the 'Land of Believers.' But as I grew older, I got to know that all religious myths told by my parents were false, and subsequently, I proclaimed myself an agnostic atheist. Atheism is the new enlightenment idea of the human species, and we will work to enlighten people about the concept of atheism. I am writing this book to expose the shortcomings of religious dogma and the evil consequences of religious indoctrinations, and why rationality is the way to progress? Many could call me Anti-Hindu or Islamophobic, but I aim to target the religions, not people affiliated with them.

The title of this book, "My Case against Religious Dogma," talks about a particular Dogma, which for centuries wrecked human intelligence. Dogma is a set of ideas or principles laid down by an authority as incontrovertibly true. Religion is not the only dogma (it can also be a political ideology like Communism) but the most menacing one, indeed.

According to the 2011 Pew Survey of India's religious affiliation, only about 30000 Indians described themselves as atheists. This book might change the statistics if you indulge in it deeply.

The question 'Is there a God?' has been asked many times by philosophers like Plato, Aristotle, St. Anselm, and many others. These philosophers used their arguments and logic to prove the existence of God.

Let's first describe a God. It is an omnipotent, omniscient, and Omni benevolent being. Atheists argue that an Omni god cannot exist. Let me explain with an example how an omnipotent being cannot exist. It is as follows-

1) God is omnipotent

2) God can make the heaviest rock (as he is omnipotent)

Now, what can we conclude with these two premises? If God is omnipotent and can make the heaviest rock. Then there are only two possibilities. First, if God is all-powerful, he can lift the rock, but this doesn't make him omnipotent as he cannot do one thing. That is, make the heaviest rock. Secondly, if God can't lift the rock, this clearly shows that he is not omnipotent. So, logically Omnipotent God cannot exist.

I want my reader to know that I will be discussing only a specific God that is an all-powerful, all-knowing, and morally perfect being.

This book's first chapter questions the existence of a creator that might have created this universe. In the second chapter, we will be discussing the problem of evil and inconsistencies of supernaturalism. We will also discuss morality and why we don't need a divine deity for the basis of morality. In the fourth chapter, we will examine how evil is religion? In a world where fake news spreads like wildfire, rational thinking is demolishing, so in the last chapter, we will discuss why empirical and critical thinking is the keys to a progressive society and why we need the idea of Secularism the most?

I am not writing this book to defame religion or harm anyone's belief. I want to challenge the faith that a believer possesses. This book is not just for an atheist but for everyone!

Finally, let me elaborate on what is atheism? Atheism is a lack of belief in a God as there is unsubstantiated evidence. There are many branches of atheism. But the type of atheism to which I am subscribed is agnostic-atheism. Agnostic atheism purports that there is no God until we get any evidence for it. Many rationalist atheists like Richard Dawkins and Christopher Hitchens advocate this particular kind of atheism (I am a part of it).

The Ten Commandments of Atheism (My creation does not apply to all atheists):

1) All religions are fake and hence should not be followed.

2) Killing is wrong, as we have agreed as a society.

3) Morality is an illusion created by humans, so have a progressive society.

4) The universe, as far as science knows, has no creator.

5) We are ready to accept the reality of a creator if the evidence is provided for it.

6) Consuming drugs and faith are injurious to our health.

7) Rationality is the way to progress.

8) Breaking someone's religious dogma is good for society.

9) Protect a nation from becoming a theocratic state.

10) Secularism should be adopted by everyone so that people can choose on their own, either religious stupidity

or scientific and rational thinking.

CHAPTER ONE

Any Proof of God?

"Isn't it enough to see that a garden is beautiful without having to believe that there are fairies at the bottom of it too?"- Douglas Adams

THE BIG BANG: A PROOF OF GOD?

The Big Bang Theory is the prevailing cosmological model that explains the existence of our universe. This theory suggests that our universe had a beginning. Our early universe was hot and dense. Big Bang was the creation of space-time and energy. The two main ways scientists predicted that our universe might have come into existence are Hubble's observation of an expanding universe and the discovery of the Cosmic-Microwave Background by Arno Penzias and Robert Wilson for which they were honored the Nobel Prize.

Many theists argue, if Big Bang was the creation of the universe, then there must be a creator who sparked the Big Bang. The major problem is that It is merely a hypothesis to say that a God is at play as there can be numerous reasons behind the Big Bang.

In 1929, Edwin Hubble made a groundbreaking discovery he discovered that the universe is expanding. He observed that all the galaxies (except Andromeda) are moving away from each other.

This discovery was revolutionary at the time and changed the perspective at which we looked at our universe. Before this discovery, scientists believed that our universe is static and eternal.

Scientists then argued to extrapolate the idea of expansion of the universe backward in time using the General Theory of Relativity yields an infinite density and temperature at a finite time in the past, this infinite density point is the gravitational singularity. At this point, all the physics of relativity breaks down.

Let's believe for the sake of argument that a God has created this universe so if God has created this universe then why this universe is so imperfect? Our universe is not perfect therefore the creator of the universe is also not perfect. Many things have no reason they are useless but still exist in our world for example the vestigial organs in humans.

Even if there is a creator of the world, he is not a perfect being which violates our assumption that God is omnipotent.

One of the major misconceptions about the Big Bang Theory is that it fully explains the origin of our universe. However, it cannot explain how energy and space-time came into existence. It only explains the emergence of the present universe from the highly dense early universe.

Big Bang cause is still not known but saying that it proves God is a fallacious argument. Big Bang Theory didn't need God to start the universe.

So what are the natural phenomena that can cause the Big Bang?

Quantum Fluctuations

In the world of quantum mechanics, quantum fluctuations can produce matter and energy out of nothingness. In quantum physics, quantum fluctuation is a temporary random change in the amount of energy at a point in space. Vacuum energy is non-zero pairs of particle-antiparticle pop in and out of existence. This shows that quantum fluctuation might be the reason behind the Big Bang. These particles are known as virtual particles, they do violate the conservation of energy but they very quickly in negligible time rejoin together as if they had never been there. Breaking the law of **conservation of energy** is theoretically allowable since the particles annihilate each other within a time limit determined by the **Uncertainty Principle.** Thus, we conclude that Big Bang is not proof of God.

Does the Universe have a Cause?

If we argue that the universe has a cause then we can also conclude that the cause is God(But this might be wrong as there could be natural causes as well but let's give the theist the benefit of the doubt) so the question is that does the universe has a cause?

Theists give us a deductive argument in favor that the universe has a cause. It is as follows-

premise1: Whatever began to exist has a cause

premise2: Our universe began to exist

Conclusion: Therefore, the universe has a cause.

Although premise2 is kind of wrong as the Big Bang Theory doesn't say that everything was created after the Big Bang only the observable universe was created and expanded. But let's believe that it is correct. But the major problem is the first premise that is whatever began to exist has a cause, here the theist is committing the fallacy of composition. Let me give an example suppose there is a wall that wall is made up of brick and the bricks are small hence the wall is also small, we all know that this is not true. It is saying like atoms are not living things therefore all things are non-living. In the same way, if all the things that we can see have a cause that doesn't mean that the universe has a cause.

THE FINE-TUNE ARGUMENT

Our universe works on natural laws. In our universe, there are four fundamental forces of nature these are - gravitation, electromagnetism, weak nuclear, and strong nuclear forces. There are fundamental constants which if get changed then can alter our universe and life will not exist. The argument is that these fundamental constants are fine-tuned for life to exist in this world.

The strength of gravity seems fine-tuned for life. If gravity has been weaker galaxies, stars and planets would not have formed in the first place. In the contrast, if gravity has been stronger, then stars would have formed from small amounts of material, which would have meant that there would have been more short-lived. This is the same with the other three forces of nature. The other possible explanation apart from God is the Multiverse hypothesis it states that there are infinite universes, and we are living in one of the infinite universes where the conditions are just right for life to exist. The other explanation is that life is fine-tuned for the conditions of our universe, not the other way around. Fine-tuning of animals can be better explained by Darwinian evolution and natural selection rather than a God. We are undermining life as we have seen life can survive in the most extreme environments. So if the physical constants change we will get a different universe but that doesn't mean that life couldn't exist in a different universe. Our knowledge of life is based on the observable and measurable phenomena that occur on Earth and is therefore limited to this instance of life. Life on the moons of Jupiter and Saturn might be different from that of Earth. It is wrong to say that the earth is fine-tuned for us, we are fine-tuned for the earth.

Another possibility is that we are living in a multiverse and that we are living in a universe where the conditions are just right for life to exist.

There is a research study that falsifies the Omni-God explanation. The conclusion of it is-

There is a cosmological constant that is a number that determines the energy density of the vacuum. It acts as a kind of pressure that, depending on its value, acts against gravity to push the universe apart or acts with gravity to pull the universe together towards a final Big Crunch.

The universe is expanding and the expansion is also accelerating, which suggests that the constant (Cosmological Constant) is positive. A positive value would tend to decrease the fraction of matter that forms into galaxies and stars which will ultimately reduce the chance of life therefore, an Omnipotent God would not choose this value and this shows that the universe is not fine-tuned for life.

Theists by proposing this argument are undermining the power of God. He doesn't need to make this whole universe for humans as most of it is inhabitable for life.

LAWS OF NATURES

We all know that our universe works upon the laws of nature, whether it be gravitation or quantum uncertainty. Science discovers these fundamental laws. So the question arises from where these laws originate? The answer is we don't know, but for a theist, the answer is God. This argument is known as the God of the gaps. It states that if something is not known by science, then there is God behind it. "If science doesn't know how these laws came, therefore God!" this type of argument is fallacious as you are not giving any evidence to back up your claim. I don't know from where these laws came from? Neither the believer knows. Maybe the laws of nature existed without any reason, but this is not testable. I can also make up an answer. For example, a turtle spits out black magic that creates the laws of nature, this is equivalent to the God hypothesis, but neither of them can be proven. A naturalist will believe that everything is governed by fundamental laws, whereas a religious person believes in a divine creature.

"I THINK THEREFORE GOD EXISTS"-ONTOLOGICAL ARGUMENT

The Ontological Argument is a philosophical argument that is used to support the existence of God. Saint Anselm of Canterbury was the first person to propose the ontological argument. His argument is as follows-

1) God is the greatest possible being that can be imagined.

2) It exists in a possible world (mind).

3) If it is the greatest being and exists in a possible world, then it should exist in all possible worlds including the actual world.

Conclusion: Therefore, God exists in the actual world.

First, as we have previously discussed an Omni God cannot exist therefore, the first statement is wrong as an Omni God is logically incoherent. Secondly, the statements are contradicting themselves, if God is the greatest being then he should not exist only in a possible world hence this reasoning is flawed. Even if we assume that this reasoning works then this can be used to prove anything like for example, a perfect island this island exists in a possible world and if this island is the perfect island, then it should exist in every possible world including the actual world.

WHAT IF YOU ARE WRONG(ATHEISTS)- PASCAL'S WAGER

"LET US WEIGH THE GAIN AND THE LOSS IN WAGERING THAT GOD IS... IF YOU GAIN, YOU GAIN ALL; IF YOU LOSE, YOU LOSE NOTHING.

WAGER, THEN, WITHOUT HESITATION THAT HE IS."- BLAISE PASCAL

The argument is what if you are wrong? What if the atheist's position is wrong and Prophet Mohammad was the last messenger of Allah? Or that Jesus was the son of God. This argument was first given by the French mathematician and philosopher Blaise Pascal. He proposed that if a theist is wrong and the atheist is right then, he will lose nothing but if a theist is right and the non-believer wrong then the atheist will suffer eternal hellfire. Therefore, it is reasonable to believe in the almighty.

This argument is a false dichotomy which means that there are more options than only two. Pascal was from the Christian faith so in his argument he gave only two options either Christianity or atheism, but it is not like that. Let's say Islam is right so if a Christian, Muslim, and atheist come at the Pearly gates God will look at an atheist as innocent as he just said I don't know if there was a God, but he will look at the Christian as a bad person, and so he deserves hellfire. Therefore, the safest person if a particular God exists is the atheist! The most outspoken atheist and a critique of Pascal's wager Richard Dawkins said that it is absurd to think that God, being just and omniscient, would not see through this deceptive strategy on the part of the "believer, thus nullifying the benefits of the wager." And lastly, this doesn't prove a God rather it is a necessary pragmatic decision that needs to be followed by every person on this planet.

Pascal was a devout Christian, and he justified his faith by logic although the logic was dead wrong.

ANCIENT ALIENS: CONSPIRACY THEORIES

Ancient Alien theorists believe that the ancient legends from different cultures were true! They think that all the mythological characters were having extraterrestrial origins like Hercules and Rama.

Theists then argue that now scientists are agreeing that God exists, but they are referring to him as aliens. This argument is absurd! First, no renowned scientist said this. Secondly, it is all speculation, Ancient Alien theorists find patterns that at first look like it has extraterrestrial origins, but it is merely speculation rather than a proof.

The theorist will look at a sculpture of a God and will immediately recognize it as a portrayal of an alien. This is known as Confirmation bias. It is a tendency to interpret and recall information in a way that supports one's prior belief. This means that you can look at the moon and can see a rabbit! But that doesn't mean anything we see what we want to see. Another example could be that in the images of Pluto we can see a heart in it. Same with constellations, the stars that make up a constellation are light years apart from each other. They do not correlate with each other and therefore, it is just a human imagination to believe that it means something.

The whole series of Ancient Aliens on History TV is utter rubbish. They misrepresent science and add creationist propaganda. But many theists use this to prove creationism and to mock mainstream science.

Look you can call the 'hell" of the bible a distinct planet like Venus but that doesn't make it right. The worst science I have seen on the show is the mercury ship which is total pseudoscience and it does not work.

Even if we don't know how the pyramids in Egypt were made (although research is still going on) that does not imply that they have any extraterrestrial origins.

Ancient Aliens are not doing science they are misrepresenting it and showing it on their program!

Evolution vs Creationism

Evolution is a biological change of a species over time. It is a theory that tells us that all the animals are related to each other and have a common ancestor. There is much evidence in favor of the theory like anatomical similarities, fossils, genetics, and geographical distribution of animals.

Creationists (Christian faith) believe that our world is just 6000 years old whereas science has estimated the earth to be 4.5 billion years old using radiometric dating. Creationists believe that the earth was flooded by a global flood, but no scientific evidence has been found in favor of it. They want us to believe that our world is just 6000 years old whereas there are pyramids older than 6000 years old.

Although this book is not about evolution I will briefly discuss the evidence that supports evolution.

Fossil Records

Fossils are remains of ancient life preserved in the ground. They are formed when a plant or animal dies in a watery environment and is buried in mud and silt. The tissues quickly get decompose and only the bones are left behind.

By scrutiny of the fossils, we can look at the ancient life that once thrived on this planet, and by radiometric dating, we can estimate how old that species was.

Scientists by studying the fossils came to realize that organisms were once different from what life we see today on earth. Although the fossil record is incomplete as only a tiny fraction of fossils have been recovered and studied by paleontologists. We have discovered fossils that have both the characteristics of the ancestral species and of the derived species they are known as *transitional fossils.*

We have also found a transitional fossil (its name is Australopithecus) that links apes like australopithecines to Homo Sapiens. This evidence shows that evolution is genuinely true and we have to consider it as a fact.

Genetics

Genes are the hereditary units that pass from one generation to another. They are made up of DNA (Deoxyribonucleic acid). They transfer the hereditary traits of both parents to their offspring.

Humans and chimpanzees share 98.8% of their DNA which makes chimpanzees our closest relatives. Surprisingly enough, humans and flies share 60% of their DNA!

These genetic similarities among different species show that they all are related and thus form the tree of life.

But the question arises, how have these different species of the past evolved to the present life we see all around us? The answer is **Mutations**.

A mutation is a change in the genetic sequence. It occurs when there are mistakes in DNA copying during cell division. It is random and happens all the time.

The new genetic variant caused by mutation is selected by the process of Natural Selection. If the new trait is beneficial for the organism then it will thrive and will reproduce to spread this new trait. If the new trait is harmful to the organism then it will not survive and the new trait will not be spread.

The most recent example was the Covid 19 virus which mutated and evolved stronger. This is a perfect example of micro-evolution. Bacteria that become resistant to antibiotics are caused by random mutations.

These are the two main pieces of evidence of evolution, and there are many more. Many creationists say that evolution is just a theory and is therefore not a fact. But, the thing is the word, "theory" is grossly misunderstood. In layman's language, it implies a guess, whereas the scientific use of the word means a set of ideas that can explain many natural phenomena backed up by evidence. Gravity is also a theory then should we also not regard it as a fact? Hell no!

CHAPTER TWO

The Problem of Evil

"To say that God permits evil in the world may not be pleasing to the ears. But if He is held responsible for the good, it follows that He has to be responsible for the evil too."- MK Gandhi

In the words of Aristotle, "Man is a rational animal." Rationality is the thing that sets us apart from the beasts. But as we glance at the history of humankind we see so much irrational stuff.

From ancient superstitions to black magic, we observe that we are not that rational. A better phrase could be, "Human is a rationalizing animal."

The Abrahamic religions which are Christianity, Islam, and Judaism all believe in one god but their customs and traditions are different. They are all based on mysticism.

If we look at science, from discovering fire to setting foot on the moon, we see a lot of progress. Science by nature is progressive. It changes as new evidence comes forward, while on the contrary, religion is as it was thousands of years ago.

Religion is based upon the faith which means belief in something without evidence whereas science is exactly the opposite of it.

Therefore, science and religion are incompatible with each other. Their ideas of finding the truth are different. One believes in faith and the other beliefs in logic and evidence. We can easily see that the most reliable one is the latter.

Naturalism is a philosophy that states everything is governed by nature and there is no supernatural. No spirits, ghosts, and God. Naturalism has many versions but the version we are discussing is the *scientific naturalism* one where only the natural laws exist nothing else.

All scientific research is based on assumptions that can be tested. These assumptions are known as fundamental laws. Naturalism believes that there is a fundamental reality and there is no creator of it and above it, is nothing.

Naturalism presumes that all the laws of nature are entirely knowable. Theories can change from time to time as evidence comes forward, but the way we do scientific research or the scientific method is unchangeable.

Ontological naturalism suggests that there no entities are influencing the physical world which is not themselves physical.

The question is which is better philosophy naturalism or supernaturalism? Supernaturalism can now only appeal to the unknown facts about our universe the questions which science cannot answer. Believers can now only pick topics that are still mysterious to science. They pick topics like dark matter, dark energy, and the cause of the big bang. These questions are still not answerable by science. The theists say they have answers for these questions, they say it is the work of God. This is known as the God of the gapes which suggests that every explanation of the unknown is the work of God.

If all question's answer is God, then how could we progress as a civilization? Edward Jenner could have said smallpox happens because it is the will of God, and if he preached this, we would not have any vaccines!

Naturalism can explain natural disasters, how an earthquake occurs, how volcanoes erupt, but supernaturalism explains this as God's will as it puts God at the top. Why would an omnibenevolent being kill its creation by a tsunami or an earthquake? This leads to the problem of evil. Why is there so much evil in society? If your God is morally perfect so why does he mercilessly kill humans all the time? The misery and the maliciousness in our world disprove an omnibenevolent God. Although there are many replies to this problem of evil, these replies by religious people have a special name *theodicy*, the most common *theodicy* is that God has given humans free will and we misuse this precious gift of God.

This theodicy is known as the theodicy of free will. It believes that God has given us free- will, but humans misuse it and cause evil. This defense can explain moral evil, but it cannot explain the natural cause of evil. Some theists will blame the natural cause of evil for the sins of humans. To them, I ask, does moral evil exist in heaven? There can be three answers that you can come up with. First, yes there is moral evil in heaven, but if there is moral evil in heaven would you call this place heaven? Secondly, no there is no moral evil existing in heaven, but then you don't have the attribute of free will which means you have no control over your actions, you are just a robot who is programmed to do good deeds. Thirdly, free will does exist in heaven, but moral evil does not, it happens by some magic. The third defense destroys the argument completely, if free will can exist without moral evil in heaven then why not on earth?

I don't think that the problem of evil is a compelling argument against God, but it is a valid one. There are many other theodicies more captivating than the theodicy of free will. There is another theodicy that explains why evil exists in our world. It states that we cannot understand goodness without experiencing bad things. So, we cannot feel happy if we don't experience sorrow. These theodicies can explain the logical problem of evil, but they cannot explain the evidential problem of evil.

The evidential problem of evil argues that God can teach us goodness by moderate kinds of evil but what we see in the world is the extreme one. Like cities destroyed by cyclones, long painful death by cancer, these things don't add anything valuable to us.

The problem of evil is dated back to the Greeks. Epicurus was the earliest philosopher who proposed the problem of evil. "Is God willing to prevent evil, but not able? Then he is not omnipotent. Is he able, but not willing? Then he is malevolent. Is he both able and willing? Then whence cometh evil? Is he neither able nor willing? Then why call him God?" – Epicurus

The problem of evil shows how inconsistent supernaturalism is. If God (assuming he exists) is not an omnibenevolent being, and he is the reason for all the suffering on earth, then why should we pray to him?

CHAPTER THREE

Morality without God

"Morality is doing what is right, no matter what you are told. Religion Is doing what you are told, no matter what is right."- H.L. Mencken

Morality is the principle concerning good and bad actions. Morals values are essential for a civilized society. Morality has changed from time to time and culture to culture. Once upon a time, slavery, racism, and sexism were pervasive, in some cases, celebrated. But today, these practices are considered abhorrent.

There is a raging debate among philosophers whether morality is objective or subjective. Objective morality is the belief that morality is universal. It means that there are moral laws like the laws of nature, and it is not dependent on us. For religious people, morals are the instructions given by God for humans to follow. On the contrary, subjective morality says that morality is the invention of humans and can vary from person to person. Although there are morals values shared by all humans, like no killing and no stealing, many morals are subjective as to whether or not they are correct. Objective morality states that killing is wrong because it is wrong, whereas Subjective morality states that killing is wrong because we agree it is wrong.

Theists believe that morality is objective, and this morality comes from God. According to Christians, the ten commandments of the bible are the foundations of morality. A common objection against atheism is that atheists cannot base morality like theists who base morality on God. This theory is known as the Divine Command theory. It suggests that we should refer to our holy books for morality.

But Plato, a Greek philosopher, objected to this theory of the Divine Command. He wrote a book on this topic, a dialogue called the *Euthyphro*. In his book, he wrote a dialogue between Socrates and Euthyphro. The two men sit outside the Athenian court. Socrates was convicted for corrupting the youth of Athens and has not had the correct beliefs of Gods. Meanwhile, Euthyphro was bringing murder charges against his father! Socrates was shocked that Euthyphro was persecuting his dad. This led to a philosophical debate between them about morality.

Euthyphro was a Divine Command theorist. He believed that the Gods commanded him to persecute his father. Plato then asked a question to Euthyphro, which we now call the Euthyphro problem. The question was –

1. Are right actions right because God commands them? Or

2. Are right actions commanded by God because they are right?

This question is a dilemma. A dilemma is a situation in which we are forced to choose two options, both leading to unpleasant results.

If you choose the first option of the dilemma then you are accepting the proposition that God commands is right because God commands them. This means that right actions are right simply because God commands them. This makes the idea of right and wrong actions vacuous.

If we choose the second option, it means that God is not omnipotent as there is one thing that doesn't come from God that is value. This also means that God has to stick to a moral book while making commands, then why can't we go to the moral book to understand morality rather than God's words.

Till now, no one has given a valid solution to the Euthyphro dilemma. This shows that the Divine Command theory is flawed.

Kantian Ethics: Categorical Imperative

18th-century German philosopher Immanuel Kant thought that morality and religion are a terrible combination, and both should be kept apart. He believed that for finding what is good or bad, we should use reason.

He believed that moral values are constant and universal. Two plus two is four for everyone either you are a Muslim, Hindu, Jain, or an atheist, it is a fact, and just like that, moral values are facts. This rule of conduct that is absolute for all agents is known as the categorical imperative.

For example, you are an office worker, and you have to attend an important meeting, but you are also hungry, and you will not get anything in the meeting room. So, you take an apple while the vendor is talking to someone else without paying. Taking a thing without paying is stealing. If you approve of this act, then you are universalizing the action that everyone should steal. This leads to a contradiction as no one would agree that everyone should steal all the time. Therefore, stealing cannot be universal, and we should not make exceptions for ourselves.

Moral values are universal was Kant's main idea. But this universalizing of morality can sometimes lead to counterintuitive situations. For example, a friend of yours comes to your house and seeks shelter from his enemies. You allowed him and started discussing the matter, and suddenly the doorbell rang, you addressed the person on the door, and the person was the enemy of your friend. He asked, "Where is your friend?", and you said he was not there. According to Kant, you should never lie not even to save your friend's life. His reasoning was: suppose you are talking to the person at the front door and you think that your friend is in a room where you have left him but, it turns out he was curious and he followed you to the door and heard the threat. In fear, he left the house from the back door. Meanwhile, to save your friend's life, you told the person he is not here. After hearing this, the person leaves and by accident runs into your friend. The blame goes to you as you told a lie and your friend got killed. If you told, the truth then according to Kant only the Killer would be the accuser.

If we take an example from the DC universe, Batman and Joker are fierce rivals. Batman is the guardian of Gotham city whereas, Joker is a criminal who terrorizes the area. Batman is always successful in catching the Joker, but he never kills him in any circumstance. Batman supports Kant's theory, as he believes that killing someone is inherently wrong in any given situation.

But some critics oppose this idea. They believe that moral laws should be based solely on the consequences of the actions rather than their intent. One theory that states this thinking is the ethical theory of Utilitarianism.

Utilitarianism

Utilitarianism is an ethical theory that prescribes actions that maximize happiness for individuals. Let me ask you a question, why do you want to choose a particular profession? Why do you want to become an artist, not an engineer? All the answers that you can come up with will lead to happiness. You do the painting because it feels good to paint. Happiness is the ultimate goal for all humans. According to this theory, good actions promote happiness and, evil acts produce unhappiness. This theory counts everyone's worth of happiness equally irrespective of their caste, sex, and religion. Therefore, a man's worth of happiness is equal to a woman's. Utilitarians agree with Kant that moral values should be equally applied to everyone, but the basis of moral values should be happiness and avoiding pain. The father of Utilitarianism is Jeremy Bentham, and later it was modified by John Steward Mill.

So far, this theory looks compelling, but if we apply it to our real world, it leads to some unpleasant actions. To understand this, let's do a thought experiment. Suppose you are a driver of a train and the rail is diverging into two paths. On one track, five workers are working, whereas on the other, only one worker is working. Reasonably, you will save the lives of five people and let the one worker die as five lives are worth more than one. Now, let's imagine a bridge across the rails. There is a fat man beside you. If you push the fat man down the bridge, then the train could stop, and you will save all six of them.

Would you push the fat man? Many people would be quite hesitant to shove the fat man as it is an act of crime, but still, it is the right thing to do. But if we assume this is true then it is a valid argument for rape. Likewise, you can use a healthy body for donating organs to multiple patients.Because of these problems, some Utilitarians came up with the theory of Rule Utilitarianism.

Rule utilitarianism suggests that we ought to live by rules, in general, that are likely to lead to the greatest good for the greatest number. Therefore, the utility of organs taken from innocent people is less where you don't have to live in fear of that happening to you. Rule Utilitarianism allows us to refrain from acts that might maximize utility in the short run and instead follow rules that will maximize utility for the long term.

After discussing some moral theories, we are sure that we can use reason as the foundation of morality. Our moral understanding has evolved drastically. Humans used to have slaves of an inferior race, and now this kind of abhorrent practice has been abolished. Religions favor these practices in the past. In the next chapter, we will be discussing how faith is the biggest curse for humanity.

CHAPTER FOUR

Curse of Faith

"Religion was invented when the first con man met the first fool."- Mark Twain

For thousands of years, religion has affected the lives of humans deeply. Religion is a set of belief systems that governs how we should live our dear lives. Almost all religions believe in the supernatural, be it an Omni-God or reincarnation.

There is no doubt that religions have shaped our way of living. If you are a Hindu, you can't eat beef. If you are a Muslim, you can't eat pork, and if you are a Buddhist, you can't consume animal meat altogether.

Imagine if someone tells you that there is a being with the highest moral character, he is the most powerful, and he can show you the right path to salvation, this vivid description of some divine being is religion. Would you believe this guy? Well, at least 84% of the total human population believes in this mysticism.

For a long time, religion has been an enemy to scientific inquiry, and we have many examples of it in history. The most famous example of religion stopping scientific thoughts is the case of Galileo. When Galileo proclaimed that the sun, not the earth is in the center of the solar system (with evidence), the Catholic Church condemned

Galileo and house arrested him. The Catholic Church convicted him as heretical.

The scientific heroes of the *Renaissance* were combating against the dogmatic Catholic Church at that time. Before Galileo, the first person to propose the heliocentric model was Copernicus. The Vaticabanned his book "On the Revolutions of the Heavenly Spheres." He famously died with his book beside him.

This shows the tyranny of the Catholic Church of that time and how it suppressed free speech and scientific endeavors. Another great martyr of free speech was the Italian philosopher *Giodano Bruno* who was burnt alive in public! He suffered this cruel punishment because he preached ideas that were different from the Church. The Catholic Church claimed to be infallible in the past, but now it admits it is fallible and has committed grave blunders in its dark past.

Religions can never be the source of morality. If you read the religious scriptures of different religions, you will find many despicable acts for the followers to follow. In Christianity, God endorses slavery and regulates it, so kind that he doesn't abolish it (sarcasm). In Islam, the punishment of apostasy is death! And in Hinduism, there is a caste system, and God has created a group of people as untouchables.

Many people say that 'all religions teach us humanity' then it will be reasonable to think that the places where people are religious should be better in terms of crime, corruption, and discrimination compared to places where people are irreligious, but in reality, is the antithesis of it. If we take countries of the Middle East and Latin America we know there are worse than countries with moderate or no religion.

Let me ask you, the reader, why do you subscribe to a particular religion? (assuming you are) Why you're a Hindu, not a Muslim? The most popular answer would be, oh, because I was born into it. Is it a valid reason to follow a particular faith? No, an individual should choose his or her faith or no faith freely, irrespective of their family's religion.

Some people brainwash their children to follow their religion without even questioning it. This nourishment of children from their birth is known as dogma. Dogma is a principle or set of principles laid down by an authority as incontrovertibly true. In the religious context, religious people nurture their children to stop questioning their faith and believe them without any other choice.

Religious dogma is pervasive in most societies. But it is very harmful to a child to live in this environment. It discourages diversity in opinion, and it suppresses the thinking of a child. To combat this, people should not impose their beliefs on their offspring.

There is a bright side to religion as well, and I don't deny it. Some religious people do charity that benefits others. For example, in the Sikh religion, the Sikh community organizes langars (serving food to everyone free of cost) that fulfill the hunger of the poor and the rich. It is a good act. Serving food is moral, but for what reason do they serve food. The reason is that they want to achieve salvation (assuming it exists). They are doing this so that God can reward them. This greed is found in every religion. In Hinduism, if you do good deeds in your life then you can attain Moksha. Greed and fear are the two main pillars of religion.

Charity by religious organizations is just a euphemism for proselytizing. Their intent is not to save the needy but to use them as an object to spread their dogmatic faith. A famous saint, who worked in India (originally from Albania), Agnes Gonxha Bojaxhiu, or more famously, Mother Teresa, has been a very highly controversial personality. She has been praised for her tremendous efforts to treat the poor by opening hospitals for them. But, many sources suggest that she was more of a bragger than a humble and kind person.

She, for her work, got millions of dollars. But, her work was not adequate compared to the massive money she received. The patients in her hospitals were not given proper care and were forcefully baptized without their consent. In, short she was a con who was made a saint. There is a famous documentary, hosted by Christopher Hitchens, showing how good of a saint she was.

Her eminent quote, "Suffering was a gift from god!" tells us how kind she was. She confessed that she was not working to eradicate poverty but convert people into Catholicism.

Religions, in most cases, oppose modern medicine that saves the lives of millions of people. Modern medicine works on research and testing and is quite reliable. But still, many people move away from modern medicine and switch to alternative medicine.

Religious leaders have discredited modern medicine for a long time. Some spoke against vaccination and claimed vaccines to be harmful, and their followers followed what they said this affects their health and causes the disease to be there in the population.

Many religious leaders organize functions in which they heal people just by spelling out incantations. All the time, the healings are just tricks and nothing else but, this makes the people believe in the magical healing.

2680927.jpg

AYURVEDA: SCIENCE OR PSEUDOSCIENCE?
(Case Study)

Ayurveda is a medical practice that started from the Indian Subcontinent. It is an alternative medicine system that is quite popular in modern India. The three main texts of the Ayurveda are Charak Samhita, Sushruta Samhita and Bhela Samhita. Ayurveda is a part of the Hindu scripture Arthveda.

Ayurveda is a very ancient medical system that dates back to 5000 years ago. Sushruta wrote the Sushruta Samhita, which is the most important treatises of the ancient world. He was the pioneer of plastic surgery and a famous gem of Indian sciences.

Many people question the credibility of Ayurveda because its model is obsolete. According to Ayurveda, humans are made up of five elements: air, water, fire, earth and ether. These elements make up the three Dosha that are-

1. Vata
2. Pitta
3. Kapha

Now, through modern medicine, we know that our body is not made of these five elements, and therefore the model of Ayurveda is incorrect. According to the 'three Dosha' theory, diseases happen when there is an imbalance in the Doshas. A bad lifestyle leads to an imbalance in the Doshas. Thanks to modern biology, we know that diseases happen because of germs that invade our bodies.

Yoga is another important aspect of Ayurveda, it is a physical and mental exercise that we do in order to stay fit physical and mentally. It originates from Ancient India and is widely practiced around the world. It has many benefits like –

1. Flexibility of the body
2. Improving the posture
3. Improves strength
4. Improves lung function
5. Many more..

Yoga is quite helpful for our bodies, but there's much pseudoscience behind yoga as well. The major criticism of yoga is that it is just an exercise and nothing else. Maybe, yoga's benefits aren't unique and any exercise will give you the same benefits. There's a lack of research done on the comparison of yoga to other forms of exercise.

There's also the spiritual side of yoga, and many people believe they can be spiritual by doing yoga and meditation. Spirituality is an ambiguous term which has no definite definition, but it has something to do with the spirit or the soul. The idea of the soul is that there is an intangible energy inside you that never dies. Well, it is all mysticism and has no scientific basis.

In conclusion, Ayurveda is pseudoscience as it doesn't follow the scientific method. It doesn't make changes in its model after examining the evidence. But, it doesn't mean that Ayurvedic medicines have no use, researches have shown that Ayurveda has some medicinal use.

For this, let me give you an example. An electric ray is an electric fish that has special glands that produce an electric current. It uses this electric current for hunting and to protect itself from predators. The Ancient Romans knew its electric property and used it to treat headaches.

Nowadays, a similar technique is used to treat migraine, but the difference is that we are using electric stimulating machines rather than electric ray fish to treat migraine. This shows that, although centuries ago people didn't know electricity and its uses still they tried something on themselves and it turns out to be useful for treatment. The 2015 Nobel Prize for medicine was awarded to Tu Youyou for her discovery of Artemisinin, which treats the disease malaria, and it was extracted from a herb used in traditional Chinese medicine. Ayurveda was around for thousands of years and, any system which is this old is bound to have something useful in its treatment.

Ayurveda is pseudoscience, but it has many uses that can be tested through clinical trials. People perceive things as either black or white but in reality things are in a spectrum of goodness, and Ayurveda comes under this strange grey region.

CULTS: The Assassins of Humanity

A cult, by definition, is a system of religious devotion towards a personality or a thing. It is a group of people that believes in strange and abnormal things that are unusual for the rest of humans. There are many weird and abysmally dangerous cults in the world.

Most of the time, the cult leaders are just bankrupts who are struggling financially and seeking opportunities to fool people and earn profit. But why do people join these kinds of groups? People join these organizations to seek answers to their personal questions. People who are not accepted in society are generally the ones who get attracted to cults.

Cult leaders are just quakes who control people by fooling them by making promises of eternal salvation or any other spiritual gibberish. They mix spiritual jargon and pseudoscience to make them look scientific.

Cults differ from religions as they are isolated from the rest of the world and the members have to adhere to a charismatic leader. Cults, by nature, are ritualistic as the members have to perform many absurd rituals to accomplish something that the cult leader has promised. Cults are a perfect example of how faith can ruin the lives of innocent people.

The most famous example of it is the Peoples Temple Agricultural Project or the Jonestown. It was a settlement in Guyana made by the Peoples Temple, a cult founded by Jim Jones. Mass murder happened at that base, and in total, 918 individuals died. According to media reports, it was a mass murder-suicide. This faith addiction caused many to lose their lives and ruined their family.

On the endnote, I would make a differentiation between faith and belief. Belief is all about logic and evidence, for example, I believe that the South Pole exists, now there is some logic behind it as the earth is a sphere, and therefore there would be a north pole and the south pole. And if you are so curious and daring. Then you can also visit that place. Faith is the antithesis of belief, as it is without logic and evidence.

CHAPTER FIVE

Hinduism: Its Myths and realities

"In Hinduism, conscience, reason and Independent thinking have no scope for development."- Dr. Br. Ambedkar

For atheists Hinduism, by far, is the toughest religion to confute. The reason behind it is the sheer complexities of its scriptures which are hard to interpret. In this chapter, I will try to make a case against the religion called Hinduism.

Hinduism is the oldest and currently the third largest religion in the world. The followers of this religion are known as Hindus. The word "Hindu" is actually a mispronunciation of the word Sindhu by the Persians. It means the people living near the Indus or Sindhu River. For this reason, some practitioners call their religion "Sanatana Dharma" or Eternal Religion.

Hinduism is a polytheistic religion as the followers believe in many deities. There is a dispute over how many Gods are mentioned in the ancient Hindu scriptures. The conundrum lies in the interpretation of the phrase 'trayastrimsati Koti' as the word 'Koti' means type and crore. The confusion is caused by the ambiguous nature of the Sanskrit language.

Reincarnation and Karma are two major beliefs in the Hindu religion. The prior, talks about the cycle of life and death and your previous life deeds dictates your present life. The latter is a concept found in most eastern religions. The Sanskrit word "karma" translates to "action." Karma's notion is that like causes produce like effects, and bad causes produce bad effects. For example, if you provide shelter to a beggar, then for that action, you will be rewarded in return for your virtuous effort.

If we look at the scientific evidence of Reincarnation, well, it is none. According to the empirical eyes of scientists, after- life is just an imagination of the human mind. But, many Hindu apologists make a point on whether we are living in a simulation or not? They support this by quoting "Sab Maya hay" or "Everything is an illusion."

The simulation hypothesis purports that the whole universe is just a creation of a computer program, and someone is controlling the world, and it could be anything aliens or God. This seems very science-fictiony analogous to the matrix, but some scientists and philosophers think that there is a high chance that we are living inside a simulation.

If we are living under a simulation, then it is plausible that God is the Hindu God and all concepts of it are true! But here's the catch, the creator of this simulation (just assuming) could be a God of any organized religion. It could a Christian God, an Islamic God or any other. It does not necessarily be a Hindu God. Therefore, even we are living under a simulation that doesn't support the ideas of Hinduism.

Now, simulating a whole universe will take a colossal amount of computing and, any civilization which can undertake such a massive task will be a very advanced civilization. With new scientific research, it has been shown that it is impossible to model the physics of our universe by any technology, whether it be alien or man-made. So we are probably not living in a simulation.

The main criticism of Hinduism is because of the idea of the caste system. The caste is a social hierarchy that divides people into four main groups. At the top of the pyramid are the Brahmans or the priest group, who are the most intelligent. And according to God, they only have the right to education. Below them are the Kshatriyas or warrior clans who serve in the army and are kings. The third one is the Vaishyas. Their occupation is mainly agriculture, cattle rearing, trade and business pursuits. The lowest on the caste hierarchy are the Shudras. They are the ones who have to serve the upper castes. They are the labour caste and are treated badly by the upper castes. The last groups which are excluded from the Brahmanical varna system are the Dalits or 'Untouchables'. They are the ones who have to carry the burden of the caste pyramid and are considered slaves by the upper castes. (Note that I am talking about 'varna' not caste. There is a difference between them. Varna is a brahaminical division whereas caste or jati is where a person is born. I have used 'caste' here but I mean 'varna' so don't get confused.)

The notion of the caste hierarchy can be traced back to the Hindu Scriptures. The most prominent Hindu Scripture that advocates the doctrines of the caste system is the Manu Smriti. The Manu Smriti or the Manava Dharmasastra is believed to be the first legal text and constitution of the Sanatan Dharma. I want to present a few of the abhorrent verses of this scripture-

1. "For the welfare of humanity the supreme creator Brahma, gave birth to the Brahmins from his mouth, the Kshatriyas from his shoulders, the Vaishyas from the thighs and Sudras from his feet."- Manu's code – I-31

2.

3. "He must never read the Vedas in the presence of the Shudras."- Manu – IV 99

4) "A Brahmina who is only a Brahman by decent, one has neither studied nor performed any other act required by the Vedas may, at the king's pleasure, interpret the law to him, act as the judge, but never a Shudra."(however learned he may be).- Manu VIII 20

5) "Any Brahmin, who enslaves or tries to enslave a Brahmin, is liable for a penalty of no less than 600 PANAS. A Brahmin can order a Shudra to serve him without any remuneration because the Shudra is created by Brahma to serve the Brahmans. Even if a Brahman frees a Shudra continues to be a slave as he is created for slavery. Nobody has the right to free him."- Manu VIII-50, 56 and 59

6) "If a Shudra arrogantly presumes to preach religion to Brahmins, the king shall have poured burning oil in his mouth are ears."- Manu VIII 272

These satanic verses are examples of the Brahminism that wants to rule the other, the so- called lower castes, in the name of God. The scripture also dehumanizes women and treat them as mere objects. The following verses show the sexist outlook of the scripture-

1. "She who disrespects to (a husband) who is addicted to (some evil) passion, is a drunkard, or diseased, shall be deserted for three months(and be) deprived of her ornaments and furniture."- Manu 9:78

2. "Wise men should never marry women who do not have marry women who do not have a brother and whose parents are not socially well known."- Manu 3:10
3. "Wise men should marry only women who are free from bodily defects, with beautiful names, grace/gait like an elephant, moderate hair on the head and body, soft limbs and small teeth."- Manu 3:11

It is pretty lucid that the Manusmriti is a scripture that advocates inequality in terms of caste and gender. The Vedas or the four main scriptures of Hinduism, too mention the caste system.

Many Hindu apologists try to make a point that the caste is not hereditary rather it is based on the innate qualities of man, and the smritis like the Manusmriti came afterwards in Hinduism by Brahamincal rulers. Well that's not true. The Vedic scriptures do point out that caste is hereditary. To prove this, let me show some a verse from the Upanishad-

1. "Those whose conduct has been good here will shortly get birth such as Brahmana(Brahamana yonim), a kshatriya, or a Vaishya. But those whose conduct has been evil will be born in evil births shortly such as the birth of a dog (shva yonim), or as a pig, or a chandala."- Chhandogya Upanishads 5.10.7

The above verse implies that the varna is decided by birth, and therefore this myth is busted.

Scientific errors in the Vedas

The Vedas are the sacred books of the Hindus. The word "Veda" literally means "knowledge." Many Hindus claim that every scientific fact and discovery is mentioned in their Vedas. From aviation technology to stem cells, all these, are mentioned in the Vedas. Unfortunately, these discoveries and inventions were looted by the Mughals or the British. Let's find out how much knowledge the Vedas possess?

There are four Vedas in number. These are -

The Rig Veda, The Yajur Veda, The Sama Veda, and the Atharva Veda. The oldest among them is the Rig Veda which was composed about 1500 BCE. It is regarded as the oldest sacred scripture.

The Vedas were written centuries ago, so the science written in it must be embryonic. But many Hindu apologists believe that the knowledge of the Vedas is a gift from the God Brahma and, it tells the truth, the only truth!

Earth is stationary according to the Vedas!

If the Vedas are the word of Brahma or the creator of this universe, then the Vedas should be infallible as a creator knows what he has created. But if we read the Vedas, then we get to find many scientific mistakes in the writings.

At the times when the Vedas were written, they didn't know the concept of moving earth, and people back then assumed that it was stationary as they couldn't feel any motion of it.

We can find many verses in the Vedas that do point to a stationary model of the Earth. The following verses will validate my claim-

"The Heavens have stood still, the earth has stood still, all creatures have stood still. The trees that sleep erect have stood still: may this disease of thine stand still!"- Atharva Veda 6.44.1

"Savitar has fixed the earth with supports, Savitar has fastened heaven in unsupported space..."- Rig Veda

10.149.1

"Indra hath fixed the earth and heaven as with an axle…"- Rig Veda 10.89.4, Sam Veda 4.1.5.8

"The heaven and earth and the mountains stands immoveable."- Rig Veda 3.30.4

The verses I have shown prove that according to Vedas, Earth is fixed!

Vedas' Geocentric Model of the Solar System

The Geocentric Model of the solar system is an outdated model which proposes that the earth is at the centre of the universe and all the heavenly bodies revolve around it. Now, we know that this model is incorrect because we have a ton of empirical evidence that debunks this model. And the heliocentric model has been accepted as the correct description of the solar system.

But the Vedas disagree with this. There are numerous verses of the Vedas backing up the Geocentric Model. This shows the scientific illiteracy of the writers who wrote them. Here are some examples-

"O, man, the sun which is most attractive, takes round of the earth, on his golden chariot through the sky and removes the darkness of the earth." – Yajur Veda 33:43

"O, Bright Sun, a chariot named harit with seven horses takes you to sky."- Rig Veda 1:50:8

The verses mention a chariot called Harit that tows the sun around the earth. So a chariot with seven horses pulls a star around a planet! That's the science of the Vedas!

Urine a remedy according to the Vedas!

"Thou art the urine of Rudra, the navel of amrita." – Atharva Veda 6.44.3

The Vedas claim that urine is a remedy for treating various illnesses! And, not only that, it is also a drink of the Gods. So, does urine has any medical properties? Well, the answer is no. There is not a single medicinal property of urine according to modern medicine. But still there are quacks who try to deceive people by making bogus claims.

Cause of rain is fire offerings?!

Every primary grade student knows the water cycle and how rain occurs, but the God of Hindu scriptures doesn't even know this. The following verse suggest that rain happens because of yagnas or fire offerings-

1. "We perform the yajnas for Vasus, Rudras and Adityas.. The desired oblation (Ahuti) reaches comes in contact with air and the light of that sun. It thence brings down rain for us.."- Yajur Veda 2.16

Flat Earth of Vedas

Flat earthers can get inspiration from the Vedas. As they, too, believe in a flat earth. Here are some verses-

1. "The ends of the earth are beheld laid waste..."- Rig Veda 7.83.3 (ends- cannot be circular right!)
2. "Thy spirit, that went far away, away to the four cornered earth."- Rig Veda 10.58.3 (four- cornered-> hmm.. like a carpet.)
3. "Great are the deeds of thee, the Great, O Agni: thou by thy power hast spread outearth and heaven."- Rig Veda 3.6.5
4. "He, having become moving majesty, went to the ends of the earth..."- Atharva Veda 15.7.1
5. "Ye raised the Sun to heaven by everlasting Law, and spread broad earth, the Mother."-Rig Veda 10.62.3

Mountains had wings according to Hindu Scriptures!

It's amusing to believe that the Gods who designed and manifested the whole reality didn't know the basics of geology. Hindu texts purport that mountains had wings to fly, but later on, Indra (the God of lightning, rain, and thunder or the Hindu version of Thor, I suppose) cut off their wings, and then, afterward, they settled down on the lands. Here's a sample of verses saying this-

1. "O son! Earlier in the Krita yuga, mountains had wings. With speed equal to that of Garuda and Vayu, they went in all direction. After that

These are the few scientific errors in the Vedas that I have mentioned. Some would argue that these verses are just metaphors and they should be taken seriously, but if that is so then there is no science in the Vedas. People who brag the Vedas haven't read them.

Sati: Brought by Mughals or written in Hindu Scriptures?

The Sati custom was a Hindu tradition in which widows were self-immolated on their deceased husband's funeral pyre. This kind of despicable practice was followed before 1829 when it was finally abolished. Raj Ram Mohan Roy, an Indian social activist, played a major role in it.

Nowadays, many people are circulating a misinformation that the Sati custom was not practiced before the Muslim invaders pillaged the country. In-fact, this tradition has been practiced since the times of the Gupta Empire. Even the Hindu scriptures avow the practice of Sati. Let me present the verses written in the scriptures.

According to Brahminism (Hinduism), there are four yugas- Satyayuga, Tretayuga, Dvaparyuga and Kulyaga.

Each yuga has its Smriti, which is applicable for only that period (yuga). Manusmriti is for Satyayuga, Gautam Smriti for Tretayuga, Shankh Smriti for Dwaparyuga and Parashar Smriti for Kalyug.

Parashar Smriti will be relevant for the present period. The practice of Sati is mentioned in the Parashar Smriti! The following verse will remove all your doubts-

"If a woman follows her departed lord, by burning herself on the same funeral pile, she will dwell in heaven for as many years as there are hairs on the human frame,-which reach the number of three crores and a half."- Verse 32 Chapter 4 Parashar Smriti

Apart from this, many other Hindu scriptures endorse the practice of Sati-

"...The widow who practices self-control and austerities after the death her husband, goes to heaven.. the widow who burns herself on the same funeral pyre with her husband also goes to heaven."- Agni Purana 222.19-23

"She then prepared a blazing fire with firewood and placed the dead body f her husband upon it. When this was finished, she lamented severely and prepared herself to perish in the fire with her husband."- Bhagwad Purana (Srimad Bhagvatam) 4.28.50

"Today itself, I too in devotion to my husband, will meet my appointed end. I shall enter the fire, duly embracing this body of my husband."- Valmiki Ramayana Ayodhya kanda 3.66.12

"...Then those Munis, practicing great vows, knew that Pandu was dead and performed duly, on the banks of the Ganges, the ceremony of burning the dead. At that time Madri gave over to Kunti the charge of her two sons and followed the Sati practice along with her husband to go to Satyaloka..."- Devi Purana 2.6.53-71

"A wife who dies in the company of her husband shall remain in heaven as many years as there are hairs on his person."- Garuda Purana 1.107.29

It is evident that the Sati practice was practiced before the advent of the Muslims. The Eran Pillar of Goparaja built in the reign of Gupta king Bhanugupta is considered to be the first mention of Sati on rock pillar.

Propaganda and fake news are trying to deceive people and is putting Indians into darkness. Hinduism is not a single unified religion but, it is an accumulation of many distinctive superstitions and practices that prevailed in the Subcontinent.

Because of these social evils in Hinduism, they got defeated at the hands of the Muslims. So, the perception of a utopian Hindu world before Islam is utterly absurd!

CHAPTER SIX

A Digression: The Aryan Migration Theory and the origin of the caste system

Inequality is intrinsic in the Brahman religion. The caste system has been the oldest social hierarchy, and it is a product of Brahmanism. But, the question arises when and how the caste system originated? This chapter is an answer to this question. We will be reviewing the Aryan Migration Theory and how it can solve the mystery of the caste system.

The Aryan Migration Theory is a very controversial topic due to the political environment. The current narrative of the Hindu Right Wing is to prove Muslims as outsiders who looted and captured India. But, to find the truth, we should look at the evidence.

The Aryan Migration Theory proposes the idea of a human migration that happened after the decline of the Harappan Civilization, from the Steppes in Central Asia to the North of India.

There is mainly three main pieces of evidence of this theory. These are-

1. Linguistic difference
2. Religious difference
3. Genetic Evidence

Linguistic Difference

Sanskrit is an Indo-European language which means it belongs to a language family native to the western and southern Eurasia. There are total 445 living Indo-European languages, mostly belonging to the Indo-Iranian branch.

One of the oldest civilizations of the world that existed in India was the Indus Valley Civilization or the Harappan Civilization. The script used in the Indus Valley Civilization (Indus script) hasn't been deciphered yet. But, many linguists have confirmed that the Indus script is proto-Dravidian, and all other Dravidian languages evolved from this script.

Surprisingly, the old Sanskrit or the Rig Vedic Sanskrit was first recorded in inscriptions found not in India but in what is now present day northern Syria. This implies that Sanskrit was not the native language of the Indians instead the Aryans brought the language to the Subcontinent.

Sanskrit was never a language of the common people, most of the time it was Pali or Prakrit languages. The study of the Vedas was also exclusive to the Brahmins. According to Manusmriti, if a Shudra even tries to listen to the recitations of the Vedas, then he shall be punished by pouring heated oil into his mouth and ears! This is also a major reason why Sanskrit came to a decline.

Route of the Aryans

Religious Difference

The Vedic Culture comprises rituals, fire offerings and offerings of animal meat to Gods. Many people claim that the knowledge of the Vedas was orally-transmitted in this period, although this claim is still uncertain. The caste system didn't start from an early age but, it began from the later Vedic period. The importance of horses and chariots is prominent in this period.

The Harappan Civilization is the earliest known urban culture that existed in the Subcontinent. It was a Bronze age civilization that dates back to 3000- 1300 BCE. The religion of the Harappans was polytheistic. Many seals excavated from the sites have shown the importance of the peepal tree and considered it to be holy. They worshipped many natural things like rivers, mountains and earth etc.

Many Historians have claimed the existence of Shiva lings in the Harappan Civilization. However, it has been strongly challenged by other historians and concluded the artifacts are something else. There are seals depicting a character that resembles Lord Shiva but this too is speculative.

Seal of a Peepal Tree

Pashupati Seal (Speculative: Lord Shiva)

Even if Lord Shiva was a God of the Harrapans still, this doesn't prove it to be Vedic as Shaivism is a small part of Hinduism, and the Aryans might have adopted Shiva as their God.

The Tradition of Building Stupas from the Harappan Civilization!

Stupa of Mohenjodaro

A Stupa is a form of architecture that is important in the Buddhist religion. It is a place where Buddhist monks meditate, and the remains of prior monks and nuns are kept. Surprisingly, the structures of Stupas predate the birth of Buddha.

Maybe, the 'concept of '28 Buddhas' is in fact true, and Siddharta was not the founder of Buddhism but a person who carried out the tradition.

The symbol of Swastika also appeared in the archaeological record of the Indus Valley Civilization. Not only that, the Swastika is even older than the Harappan Civilization! The symbol of Swastika symbolizes peace and continuity. Adolf Hitler also used this symbol with a little twist to back up his Aryan Supremacy Theory.

The Quest of Horses and Chariots in Indus Valley Civilization

As I have already mentioned, horses were ubiquitous in the Vedic Period. But, the evidence of them in the Harappan Civilization is bare minimum or literally zero. Horses are not native to the Subcontinent but still we can find many descriptions of horses in the Vedas.

The significance of horses in the Vedic times and the absence of them in the Harappan Civilization proves that horses came from outside and later became a part of the Vedic tradition.

Though, there are a few archaeological findings that confirm the presence of horses. These findings are vigorously challenged by contemporary historians. Even if we approve these findings, horses were imported from other civilizations that can explain the presence of horses at the sites.

Genetic Evidence

The strongest evidence, so far, for the Aryan Migration Theory is the genetic evidence. New genetic evidence is upholding the claim of the Aryan Migration Theory. This new research has found the prevalence of Ra1 in India, which is robust proof that there was a migration from the Steppe Region of Central Asia to India.

The Brahmins are to be found with the most Steppe Ancestry among the population of India. It can somehow explain the origin of the caste system.

When the Aryans entered India, they mixed with the local population living there at that time. But, at some point, they stopped intermingling with each other and then, they started practicing endogamy.

This can also be verified as the caste system was not there in the Early Vedic Period but started from the Late Vedic Period. This is also the reason why Manusmsriti denounces inter-caste marriage so that people would marry in their caste. The imagination of racial purity and its superiority has devastated humanity throughout history.

Overall, the Caste system was implemented to control the indigenous population of the Subcontinent. Religion has been used for many evil things. From justifying killing to ruling an entire country, every answer to these questions can be answered by religion and their God.

CHAPTER SEVEN

Holy Wars: Religion against Peace

"Religion is the sigh of the oppressed creature, the heart of a heartless world, and the soul of the soulless conditions. It is the opium of the people."- Karl Marx

"We all remember how many religious wars were fought for a religion of love and gentleness; how many bodies were burned alive with the genuinely kind intention of saving souls from eternal fire of hell." – Karl Popper

Religious leaders and saints often pretend religion to be peaceful, and the problem is with the people, not with faith. This cliché has been used from time to time when riots and battles happen in the name of God.

The God of the Gita, Krishna, instructs Arjuna to kill his cousins solely over a property dispute. If Krishna is a God, then why couldn't he solve the issue with his omnipotent powers? In the same way, the God of the Bible condones the most abhorrent act of slavery. Similarly, the God of the Quran will kill every non-believer by sending that person into eternal hell-fire. The Gods of different religions seem very brutal towards their human slaves.

But, in contrast to all of this, there are examples of a few saints and pious social workers who confronted religious violence and religious bigotry. For example, Gandhi was an idealist saint. He went to protest against the violence that was happening during the partition of India. He stood up for the Hindu-Muslim fraternity and was against the two-nation theory supported by the communal parties (Muslim League and the Hindu Mahasabha). Another saint from medieval India was Kabir Das. He was a prominent poet from India and he too stood for Hindu-Muslim unity.

These examples could easily show that the fault is not in the precepts of religion but the nature of man. But, as I have already mentioned, these textbooks of religion are war books written by people with vicious intentions.

Religion, from time to time, has facilitated war. But, battles don't happen solely because of religious faith but, both sides in conflict use religion as an excuse for warfare as they will get some political or economic gain.

The most famous examples of religious wars in history were the Crusades. The Crusades were a series of military expeditions, started from the 11th century, by the Western European Christians against Muslim rule.

The main motives of the Crusades were to retake the Holy Land of Christians Jerusalem, recapture the formerly Christian territories and capture surrounding areas.

The Crusades were the religious battles among the Three Monotheistic faiths Christianity, Islam and Judaism. The soldiers participating in the war were promised that they would get to heaven if they would fight for their religion. This greediness turned to be useful as they mobilized massive troops by just telling the soldiers that God was with them.

If we go by statistics, in total, only 6.98% of the total wars that occurred in human history have their primary cause as religion. This seems to be that religion is not a significant cause of conflict, and that's somewhat true, but if we look at the teachings of different faiths, at the crust, they try to show that they are peaceful, but from inside, there are violent.

For example, if we examine the teachings of Islam the verses of the Quran are contradicting themselves, like the surah 5 verse 32 says- "If anyone kills a person, it would be as if he killed the whole people: and if anyone saved the life of the whole people."The teaching of the verse is pretty clear- "Don't kill", but we see people with arms chanting "Allah uh Akbar" violating this verse? So, are they Un-Islamic, well no, actually they are the one who are liberally interpreting the Quran. Let me show you some violent verses- (Surah in Arabic is synonymous with a chapter)

1. "But when the forbidden 4 months are past, then fight and slay the pagans whenever you find them, and seize them, beleaguer them, and lie in wait for them in every stratagem (of war); but if they repent, and establish regular prayers and practice regular charity, then open the way for them: for Allah is Oft-forgiving, Most Merciful."- Quran 9:5-5

2. "We will cast out terror into the hearts of those who disbelieve for what they have associate with Allah of which He had not sent down authority. And their refuge will be the Fire, and wretched is the residence of the wrongdoers."- Quran Surah 3 Verse 151

3. " Indeed, those who disbelieve in Our verses- We will drive them into a fire. Every time their skins are roasted through, we will replace them with other skins so they may taste the punishment. Indeed, Allah is ever Exalted in Might and Wise."- Surah 4 Verse 56

4."O Prophet, urge the believers to battle. If there are among you twenty (who are) steadfast, they will overcome two hundred. And if there are among you one hundred (who are steadfast), they will overcome a thousand of those who have disbelieved because they are a people who do not understand."- Surah 8 Verse 65

5. "Fight against in those who do not believe in Allah or in the Last Day and who do not consider unlawful what Allah and his Messenger have made unlawful and who do not adopt the religion of truth (a.k.a. Islam) from those who were given the Scripture – (fight) until they have given jizyah (tax on non-Muslims) willingly while they are humbled."- Verse 29 Surah 9

6. "O Prophet, strive against the disbelievers and the hypocrites and be harsh upon them. And their refuge is Hell, and wretched is the destination."- Surah 66 Verse 9

After looking at these verses, no one could ever say that Islam is a religion of peace. Many Muslim reformers have tried to remove these *sword verses* from the Quran as it instills hatred towards other faiths in the people's minds. But, the Islamic world has never accepted the need to reform as they think that the Quran is the last revelation by God and no change is needed.

The Islamic State and other terrorist groups around the world use religion as their tag mark for violence. The person who hijacked the plane during the 9/11 attack was on the opium of faith. He was dreaming about going to Jannah or Heaven by taking the lives of innocent people. This is what religion does to a man. It makes him a self exploding bomber!

Though Islam plays a big part in spreading the words of savagery, other religions, too, have their kinds of violent indoctrinations. Hinduism is thought to be peaceful and tolerant, but as I have debunked the many other claims of Hinduism this, too, I will debunk.

The majority of the people think that Hinduism is one of the most tolerant religions in the world, and any concept of Blasphemy doesn't exist in Hinduism. But, if we dig deep into their sacred books, we will find that it is not the case.

I will be quoting few verses from the Vedas to prove my claim-

1. "May you (O love Divine), the beholder of the path of enlightenment, purifying our minds and destroying the infidels who refuse to offer worship, come and stay in the prime position of eternal sacrifice."- Rig Veda 9.13.9
2. "May the fire divine chase away those infidels, who do not perform worship and who are uncivil in speech. They are niggards, unbelievers, say no tribute to fire divine and offer no homage. The fire divine turns those godless people far away who institute no sacred ceremonies."- Rig Veda 7.6.3
3. "May Agni (fire) burn the God- denying demon: let no carnivorous. Pisicha drink here. We drive him off, we keep him at a distance. Adityas and Agirases pursue him."- Atharva Veda 12.3.43
4. "O light-divine and plasma-divine may you exterminate those who strive against you and break the laws that are agreeable and beneficial and also those divinites, and mortals, who are not diligent in adoration, and those who work without faith and those who performing works do not worship and those who do not propitiate you."-Rig Veda 6.67.9

The above verses target the infidels and atheists who do not believe in the Vedas. This indicates the resentment towards the non-Vedic people who were Buddhists, and Jains at that time.

Buddhism was another major religion in the subcontinent, and it co-existed with Brahaminsim (which is present-day Hinduism).

The ideas of Buddhism are atheistic, and Buddha himself denied the existence of any God. The Brahmins, on the other hand, believed in Gods and their avatars, so they started condemning Buddha. Sometimes, they will declare Buddha as an avatar of Lord Vishnu, and, sometimes, they will criticize Buddha and call him the devil.

The Puranas are the Hindu texts which have mentioned Buddha many times. The following verses explicitly condemns Buddha and its religion-

1. "Asuras, the enemies of the celestials, became proficient in the knowledge of the Vedas, and having got made by Mayadanaba (an Asura of that name) and invisible city of velocity, engaged themselves in the destruction of the people. Thereupon the glorious God incarnated Himself as Buddha, and with a view to bring about a confusion of their understanding and to create avarice in them taught them many _False religions._"- Srimad Bhagavatam 2.7.37

2. "Then, in the beginning of Kali-yuga, the Lord will appear as Lord Buddha, the son of Anjana, in the province of Gaya, just for the purpose of deluding those who are envious of the faithful theist."- Srimad Bhagavatam 1.3.24

3. "..Some of them began to mark on their bodies various heretical signs, e.g., Taptamuda, etc.; some became Kapalikas; some became Kaulas; some Buddhas and some Jainas. Many of them, though learned, became lewd and addicted to other's wives and engaged themselves in vain and bad disputations. For these, they will have to go again surely to the _Kumbhipaka Hell._"- Devi Bhagvatam 12.9.91-100

The notion of 'False Gods' has been attributed to Abrahamic religions, but in Hinduism, too, it exists!

The Abrahamic religions proclaim that their religion is the true religion, and the disbelievers will go to hell for not incessantly adoring their religion. The same case is with Hinduism, for that matter.

"Those who have ceased to perform the rites and the yajnas for Pitrs (manes) and Devas, those who stay outside the part of the Vedas, are notorious as heretics. They undergo all sorts of torture."- Narada Purana I.15.130b-131a

This verse from the Narada Purana shows the blatant restriction on apostasy. And the non-Vedic (believing in another religion) people will dwell in eternal Hell.

The hatred towards Buddhism is so much that even stepping foot in a Buddhist place is a sin.

"There is no expiation anywhere to those persons who intimately associate themselves with Sudra women, whose bodies are nourished with the food of the Sudras and who indulge themselves in denouncing the Vedas. There is no expiation here or hereafter to those who find fault with stories of saintly people. Even through hundreds of expiations, it is impossible to see the redemption of that Brahmana who enters a Buddhist shrine, even in a great emergency. The Buddhists are heretics, as they are the revilers of the Vedas. Hence, a Brahmana shall not even look at them, since they are excluded from righteous holy rites. A Brahmana may enter a Buddhist shrine knowingly or unknowingly. If he enters knowingly, there is no redemption at all. This is the decision of the Scriptures."- Narada Purana I.15.49-53

Hinduism is not an exceptional religion as it is perceived by the general public. It has the same narrow-minded and regressive indoctrinations as all other organized religions. Hindu Extremism is rampant in present India. In India, a mob can chastise a Muslim for eating Beef. Cow lynching and continuous violence against the Indian minorities shows the bigoted nature of Hinduism. We should remember that the first terrorist of post-independence India was none other than a Hindu.

No religion is immune to extremism, whether Islam or even the most peaceful religion, Buddhism. In Myanmar, which is predominantly a Buddhist majority state, Rohingya Muslims are being persecuted by the same faith, which advocates pacifism (although the basic tenets are non-violent. But when politics, religion, and racism mix together, things go wrong).

Why Islam is the most Intolerant Religion? A Retrospection on Islam.

The word 'Islam' means submission to the will of God. Nowadays, the word Islam is synonymous with Terrorism.

But why is it so? Why it is the most intolerant religion among all religions? To find out, we have to retrospect the History of Islam.

The origination of Islam started with one man in Arabia, and that man was Muhammad. Apart from being religious leader, he was also a political leader. Hence, to spread his message of Islam, he used violence as a medium.

In history, Muhammad was not a peaceful prophet who established Islam by persuading the people of Arabia, but he was a warlord who spread Islam on the sword. Before the advent of Islam, the Middle East was full of polytheistic myths which have their roots in the Mesopotamian myths.

The Historicity of Muhammad is undoubted as we have tons of evidence that a person called Muhammad lived in Arabia, unlike Jesus and Moses. The life of Muhammad is full of conquering and bloodshed. His conflict against the polytheists, which he called *Kafirs,* shows his arrogance as a religious leader.

If we compare him to Jesus (although his historicity is doubted), Jesus was not a person who went to battle just because someone disagreed with him. He spread his message not by violence but by persuasion.

The Muslims have to imitate their beloved prophet. Because of this, Islam is synonymous with terrorism. Its foundation is built upon violence. Its punishment for apostates, resentment of non-believers, oppression of women, and the other types of tribalistic justice is problematic.

Apostasy or the formal disaffiliation from religion is a heinous crime as per Islamic law. The punishment for apostasy in Islam is straight away death! Millions of ex-Muslims in the Middle East and even in Europe strive against the Muslim radicals and, in the case of the Middle

East, against the governments.

Another salient reason is that Islam claims to be the last and the final message sent by God or Allah, and they do consider the Judeo-Christian prophets but by going one step forward to claim that Muhammad was, too, a messenger of God. This puts it in a rather challenging position to change or reform. But this doesn't mean that, so far, no reformation has taken place in the religion of Islam. The "Sufi" version of Islam is relatively peaceful and benign compared to the original one. And they sing! (Which is haram or prohibited by Islam)

Islam is relatively a new religion and currently the most obnoxious and violent form of religion, of the present times. I suppose every religion is dangerous to humans. For instance, If I were writing this book in the 12th century CE during the advent of the Spanish Inquisition, I would have opined the Catholic Church to be the most tyrannical form of religion. The point is that in different periods different religions rise in terms of violence and savagery, and this era is the era of Islam.

Religion is dangerous for humanity, and its end is inevitable!

CHAPTER EIGHT

Why God is Against Women?

Patriarchy is all around the world. In most parts of the world, women are still not considered equal. But, now the advent of democracy, this patriarchal thinking of people is slowly changing, and in future, we will have an ideal world where women can have the same rights as a man on the ground.

Religions have existed for centuries like patriarchy, and anyone would expect it to solve the problem of patriarchy? But it didn't, and, on the contrary, they sanctioned the act of patriarchy!

Every religion, in sort of a way, has discriminated against women. Islam is the worst in this. The recent Taliban annexation of Afghanistan has caused rampant discrimination against women. They were kicked out of their jobs. They were forced to cover their bodies by hijab and burqa. The Taliban is doing nothing new as it is written in their holy books, and there are, implementing what's written.

Islam and women rights are incompatible. To highlight my argument, let me present you some verses from the Koran and the Hadiths (description of the life of Prophet

Muhammad)-

1. "Your wives are a tilth for you; so go to your tilth when or how you will..."- Quran 2:223

2. Narrated by Abu Sa'id Al-Khudri: the Prophet said, "Isn't the witness of a woman equal to half of that of a man?" The woman said, "Yes." He said, "This is because of the deficiency of a woman's mind."- Sahih al-Bukhari 2658

3. "Men are in charge of women, because Allah hath made the one of them to excel the other, and because they spend of their property (for the support of women). So good women are obedient, guarding in secret that which Allah hath guarded. As for those from whom you fear rebellion, admonish them and banish them to beds apart, and scourge them. They if they obey you, seek not a way against them."- Quran 4:34

These verses show the misogynist outlook of Islamic texts. The third verse straight away permits to do domestic violence. Many apologetics try to get away by changing the translation and the interpretations, but there are easily caught.

The blatant discrimination against women shows the synthetic nature of religions. This proves the statement that "Man makes God and not the other way around." The God of Jesus has, too, no plans for giving women their equal rights.

1. "Let the woman learn in silence with all subjections. But I suffer not a woman to teach, nor to usurp authority over the man, but to be in silence. For Adam was first formed, then Eve. And Adam was not deceived, but the woman being deceived was in the transgression."- 1 Timothy 2:11-14 (New Testament)

2. "I do not permit a woman to teach or to exercise authority over a man; rather, she is to remain quiet." – 1

Timothy 2:12

3. "Wives, be the subject to your husbands as you are to the Lord. For the husband is the head of the wife just as Christ is the head of the church."- 1 Corinthians 14:34-35

Exploitation and oppression are the two main benefits religious rulers get from religion. That's why we need freedom from the mental slavery of religion!

Like Abrahamic religions, Eastern religions are no different. Hinduism is as bad as the Abrahamic religions in terms of women's rights. The Manusmriti (I know this book sucks) is quintessential of this-

1. "Women have no divine right to perform any religious ritual, nor make vows or observe a fast. Her only duty is to obey and please her husband and she will for that reason alone be exalted in heaven."- Manusmriti 5.158

2. "It is the duty of all husbands to exert total control over their wives. Even physically weak husbands must strive to control their wives."- Manusmriti 9.6

3. "While performing namkarma and jatkarm, Vedic mantras are not to be recited by women, because women are lacking strength and knowledge of Vedic texts. Women are impure and represent falsehood."- Manusmriti 9.18

4. "One should not marry who has have reddish hair, redundant parts of the body (ex- six fingers), one who is often sick, one without hair or having excessive hair and one who has red eyes."- Manusmriti 3.8

5. "A Brahman, true defender of his class, should not have his meals in the company of his wife and even avoid looking at her. Furthermore, he should not look towards her when she is having her meals or when she sneezes or yawns."- Manusmriti 4.43

These so-called "Holy" books are in no sense holy. Burning these books will be the betterment of the human species.

CHAPTER NINE

The Concept of Blasphemy vs Free Speech

"The crime called Blasphemy was invented by priests for the purpose of defending doctrines not able to take care of themselves."- Robert G. Ingersoll

Speech is a way of conveying our thoughts to others. Since the dawn of human civilization, we have been using speech as a way to communicate. Therefore, it has existed for millennia. But, the concept of 'free' speech is a new one. Its origin comes from the first amendment of the US constitution (it happened in 1791) which, protects the freedom to express one's thoughts wishfully,

Free speech is a fundamental human right recognized by the United Nations. It guarantees an individual to express his thoughts willingly. Although, it's not an absolute right as some restrictions are on it. If an individual crosses the threshold line then, it is reckoned to be 'Hate Speech.'

If we go by the Oxford dictionary, the definition of Hate Speech is "abusive or threatening speech or writing that express prejudice against a particular group, especially on the basis of race, religion or sexual orientation." For example, if I target a particular community and belittle them subsequently, it's considered Hate Speech.

Blasphemy is very different from Hate Speech. Blasphemy is a religious crime of insulting the religious faith and sentiments of the people. It is looked on as contempt or disrespectful of religious deities and saintly rituals.

Blasphemy in the present time exists in about 71 countries out of 195. Thirteen countries are such where capital punishment is awarded to Blasphemers. The thirteen countries are – 1) Afghanistan, 2) Iran, 3) Malaysia, 4) Maldives, 5) Mauritania, 6) Nigeria, 7) Pakistan, 8) Qatar, 9) Saudi Arabia, 10) Somalia, 11) Libya, 12) The United Arab Emirates and 13) Yemen. (Note- in India, too, blasphemy law exists on paper. It is according to Section 295(a) of the Indian Penal Code)

All these countries are Islamic, and for that matter, repudiating Islam is also a heinous crime according to their Sharia Law. Blasphemy in Islam is the most stringent one among all other religions. The prime example of this is the Charlie Hebdo shooting. Charlie Hebdo is a French satirical magazine that features cartoons pertaining to religion and politics.

The controversy sparked because of a cartoon published by Charlie Hebdo magazine. It was a cartoon on Prophet Muhammad. According to many Islamic interpretations, depicting the prophet's image is forbidden. And a cartoon of him would inevitably go against the Islamic laws.

(Above image) Map of Countries having Blasphemy laws in their law book.

In reaction to the cartoon, a series of terrorist attacks shook French soil in January 2015. A mere caricature of a historical figure wreaked the country with terror. Islam is solely the biggest reason for blasphemy around the world. But, blasphemy exists in almost every religion.

Arguments for Blasphemy

The right-wing groups around the world have supported the blasphemy laws. They have a few arguments in support of it. Let's check it, one by one-

Faith is a serious deal!

Blasphemy's main argument is that 'Faith is a serious deal.' Interfering in faith is not good. This is the premise of the right-wing, and therefore blasphemy laws should also exist.

Giving faith a high value is quite dubious. Having faith in something means that you believe in something that has no proof. So, in the physical world, faith has no value. Faith is the cannabis of society and cannot be valued.

For instance, the right-wing gets offended by the cartoons of mythical creatures. They argue that making cartoons on Muhammad is wrong because the Muslims love him more than his parents. They commit the logical fallacy of equivalence and emotion by comparing Muhammad or any mythical god with their parents. Muhammad was a historical figure, and making cartoons on him is nothing wrong, just like anyone can make cartoons on Abraham Lincoln and Akbar. Likewise, cartoonists can make caricatures of God or goddesses as they can insult the character of Superman.

Blasphemy is Hate Speech

It is the most feeble argument put forward by the right-wingers. As I have already mentioned, Hate Speech and Blasphemy are two very different things. Hate Speech is to target a particular community. And that's called racism. But, blasphemy is a criticism or insult to the tenets of a religion.

For instance, if I insult the God Krishna of Bhagavata Gita. Then that could be considered Blasphemy. But, if I enounce against the Hindu community, that's hate speech. Distinguishing hate speech and Blasphemy is a necessary step to be taken by all legislations around the world.

Why we don't this law in the 21ˢᵗ century?

Blasphemy laws mainly revolve around the idea of 'sacred things or ideas.' But, how do we define anything to be sacred? For a Christian, the Bible is sacred. For a Muslim, the Koran is holy, and for a Hindu, Gita is divine. It shows the subjectivity of so-called "sacred" things.

Societies have evolved, and now the notion of a "sacred" thing is becoming superfluous. People are now becoming more tolerant of other people with different views. "No idea is sacred" that's the motto of the 21st-century enlightenment. If a person can criticize a political leader, why not the God of Gita or Koran?

Another point against Blasphemy is that it ceases the space to reform. Reformation in religions is necessary with time, but with the Blasphemy laws, no one can touch the topics of religion as that person would then be a Blasphemer. For instance, Raja Ram Mohan Roy, a social reform (a firm believer), spoke against the Sati custom. But, the people back then could have called him a Blasphemer, and the Sati custom wouldn't have been abolished.

A further problem with Blasphemy is that it creates strife among different religious communities. For example, in many states of India, cow meat is taboo and is banned by the law, and the reason for it is that cows are considered "holy" by the Hindus, and their meat is forbidden. But the Muslims have no problem eating beef, but still, they are restricted.

Because of this law, many radical Hindu organizations target Muslims and take the law into their hands. It's reasonably evident that Blasphemy laws can be used against the minorities of a nation.

Blasphemy comes under Free Speech, and everyone has the right to criticize and insult the mythical fantasies of the masses. Therefore, these garbage laws around the world

which infringe the fundamental right of free speech should
be repealed!

CHAPTER TEN

Astrology: The Godfather of all Pseudoscience

"Dictators seek to control men's thought ... and so they attempt to dictate science, education and religion. But dictated education is usually propaganda, dictated history is often mythology, dictated science is pseudoscience."- Edwin Grant Conklin

Astrology is pseudoscience, and Astronomy is science. This one sentence could finish this whole chapter. But the aim of writing this chapter is to tell the absurdness of this field of pseudoscience. It's a story of how irrational humans were, and now, with the help of science and reasoning, we are moving towards the path of supreme rationality.

Astrology is a practice of foretelling the future through observing the night sky. It was popular in ancient times.

Besides that, hand telling, alchemy, and black magic were also prominent. Nowadays, in the information age, these fraudulent practices still exist.

Indians are the most dogmatic in believing astrology. According to the Pew survey, nearly 44% of Indians believe in the rubbish myth of astrology, and of which 49% percent are Hindus (they are the biggest group in believing astrology).

Astrology always has been given a soft corner in India. Media has a big role in this. You will find horoscopes in newspapers and TV news channels. If we want to end this superstition, we have to enlighten the general population that astrology is a delusion.

The invention of Astrology is credited to the Babylonian Civilization in the 2nd millennium BC. The Babylonians were the first people to invent horoscopes. They were the first to connect the motion of heavenly bodies with the obscure life of a person. From there, it spread to the Hellenistic world and then to India.

It's a big misconception that astrology was native to India. But it came from Greece. The traditional Hindu astrology is known as Jyotish. The earliest treatise on Jyothish was the Brigu Samhita, written by the sage Brigu during the Vedic period.

Now, let's deal with the question, is astrology a science? For this, let's see the model of the solar system purported by astrology. According to Hindu astrology, there are nine planets. They are-

1. Sun
2. Moon
3. Mars
4. Mercury

5. Jupiter
6. Venus
7. Saturn
8. Rahu (it's not a real planet. It is a mythological one.)
9. Ketu (this, too, fictional)

This is the hilarious model of Vedic astrology! Now, we know it's not true as there is a total of 8 planets, not nine. Sun is not a planet but a star, like trillions of others that we see at night. Rahu and Ketu are mythical planets. Rahu was a deity that was beheaded by the Gods and, then it flies off in the sky and swallows the sun! And that's how solar eclipses occur! But, science has proven that a solar eclipse occurs when the moon casts its shadow on the earth. Science has explicitly destroyed the belief of Hindu astrologers, and these are the people who tell you the future of yours, but they don't even have the basic knowledge of our solar system.

There's also a common practice of fearing solar eclipses, and cultures around the world consider solar eclipses to be a bad omen. Although in the west, this superstition is vanishing in the east, this fear is very much there. I remember the time when my parents stopped me from going outside as a solar eclipse was setting in. At that time, I tried to persuade them that this was just a delusion, but they refused. Many other Indians may connect this story with their lives. This happens when religious dogma rules the country in every aspect of life.

It's quite humorous to believe that planetary motions could ever affect the lives of ordinary people. But still, many studies have tested the validity of horoscopes and how accurately they predict the future of someone's life. The results were a plain flop.

If astrology is total bogus then, why do people believe in this? People tend to believe these things when they are depressed. They might have lost a closed one or have failed an exam. These factors could lead a person to astrology. For them, it's the thing that gives them hope and gets addicted to this insobriety.

Many people could argue that astrology, though it's a pseudoscience, is harmless or benign. Why should we care about a person who goes to an astrologer to seek his advice? It's not true. Pseudoscience can get very harmful. This is because when the majority or a large portion of the society subscribes to this pseudoscience, it dims their ability to use logic and reason. It decreases the scientific literacy of the people. It throws them back to the dark ages.

It can get even worse if a ruling government or a regime uses this pseudoscience to administer their states. A country could attack another country just because a priest insisted they do so. A priest could even initiate a nuclear war solely on his pseudoscientific knowledge. Overall, any type of pseudoscience, whether it be black magic or astrology, could stifle humanity's scientific thinking.

CHAPTER ELEVEN

Mythology against Science

"Religions are all alike- founded upon fables and myths."-Thomas Jefferson

What are myths? Myths are the traditional stories that have a cultural connection with religion. They are fictitious stories depicting supernatural beings or Gods. Though they have no historical evidence, still believers of all faiths believe in these mythical fairy tales. Hindus believe in their Lord Rama and Krishna, Muslims believe that Prophet Muhammad split the moon into two parts, and the Christians believe that the whole earth got deluged by a global flood and Noah's ark!

As science is debunking all these claims, some apologetics are trying to justify their claims by manipulating and misrepresenting facts. They are using the same 'science' which they hate the most.

When internet access is around the world, these people (apologetics) are spreading misinformation about science, some debunking evolution, and some the Big Bang! Let's see what they have got?

Noah's Ark and the Great Flood! (claim by Christianity)

The story goes with a man named Noah. He was a good man who feared God and acknowledged him as the greatest. Others all around him were wicked and selfish. Because of this, God got angry and decided to flood the whole earth!

He chose Noah as the right man to repopulate the planet again. So, he commanded him to make a large boat that was one and a half football-size long! His neighbors were laughing at him as they thought he was a psycho. How can there be a flood in this desert land? They argued. But, he did what God had commanded.

God also instructed him to collect pairs of all the creatures of the earth and embark them with him. Finally, rain struck the land and flooded the planet. All beings died except those who were there on the ark boat. Noah and his crewmates then disembarked the ship and repopulated the land. Noah prayed to God to never flood the planet again. God agreed and created a rainbow, a promise that he would never flood the earth again!

This is a brief story of Noah's ark (It is mentioned in Genesis chapters 6-9). Many Christian apologetics especially, Ken Ham, has claimed it to be true. A debate was held between Bill Nye, a science communicator, and Ken Ham, a young-earth Creationist. In that debate, Bill Nye brutally deflated all the arguments put forward by Ken for the Noah's ark tale.

Many sites on the internet like the answers in genesis are spreading this propaganda that there is evidence for the Noah's ark. There is zero evidence of the Noah's tale.

But still, here are some reasons why the Great flood and Noah's ark never happened –

1. The feasibility of constructing a massive ship which is written in the Bible with full detail at that time is

impossible.

2. Another point that goes against the story is that when this kind of shipbuilding was developed just after the catastrophe, there was no advancement in shipbuilding. They went back to the old technique of hollow logs and simple designs. It didn't make any difference in shipbuilding which makes it ridiculous.

3. How can a person cram all the species of planet earth into one single boat?

4. The whole story originates from a book that has no historical credibility.

Ramayana: A tale of history? (claim by Hinduism)

The epic of Ramayan is considered to be 'itihas' or history by Hindus. However, the historical events of the epic are still debated among historians. Many, who claim that Ramayana is not myth, point out many archaeological pieces of evidence backing up the story of the epics.

In this part, I will be examining the shreds of evidence put forward by believers, and I will be debunking them all!

Ram Setu: The Bridge created by the army of Rama?

Ramayan is a story of a hero (Rama) whose wife has been abducted by a demon, King Ravan. Rama, then, starts on a journey to Lanka, where he defeated Ravan and took her wife back to his kingdom.

But, to reach Lanka, he and his army had to cross the sea, so they built a bridge by throwing rocks. Some people speculate that the Adam's Bridge is the same bridge mentioned in the Ramayana.

Adam's Bridge is a collection of coral reefs. Corals are marine animals that form colonies that are known *as Coral Reefs. The Adam's Bridge is a long chain of coral islands.* Hence, it is a naturally occurring phenomenon rather than a man-made bridge.

India and Sri Lanka are connected by land, but due to rising sea levels, the landmass got submerged into the seas. Between 18,000 to 7000 years ago, the connection would have been visible. But, as the glaciers started to melt, it caused an increase in the sea level.

Now let's talk about the age of the Adam's Bridge. There is an uncertainty of its age, but geologists put it in the time limit of 125,000 years to 3,500 years. If we believe in Ramayana myth as history, we also have to acknowledge that Ramayana happened, at the end of the treta yug, 950000 years ago. But, at that time, no human was there on earth, so how could Ramayana take place?

Astronomical data of Rama & other characters of Ramayana

Many believers claim that the astronomical data of Rama and other characters written in Ramayana are proven true by computer software. I will be debunking this claim by scrutinizing the findings that the believers are referring to.

There is a loophole in this finding. The planetarium software that they are referring to is "Planetarium Gold". This software cannot calculate astronomical positions that are before 3000 BC. By its calculation, the information that we have got is that Saturn was in Taurus zodiac rather than in Libra zodiac (contradicting the Ramayana), another software used to do calculations which was ejplde 431 software which differs from the result of the previous one. Hence, the data from the planetarium software is misleading, and it does not prove Ram's birth date.

Now, if we keep this aside, still there is one problem. The astrology and zodiac, written in Valmiki's Ramayana, was introduced by the Greeks, then how could Valmiki write it thousands or millions of years ago?

According to believers, their Brahamincal scriptures were written thousands of years ago, so I want to ask them which script (lipi) is used to write these books? The answer would be Devnagiri, but Devnagiri script is there from 1st to 4th century CE then, how can these books be older than 1st century CE?

Not, even that, if we read the notes of the foreign traveler Al Beruni, he has mentioned that the Brahmins did not write the Vedas instead, they transmitted the knowledge orally. He came to India in the 11th century. This makes it pretty clear that the Vedas and other writings weren't before the 11th century CE! (Note- The oldest manuscript of Rig Veda is of 1464 AD)

CONCLUSION

Ramayana, for historians and rational people, remains a myth. If we have to prove something in history, we need to have two types of evidence, either literary or archaeological evidence. For Ramayana, the archaeological proof is none, and neither does literary. We cannot take the Ramayana book as literary history because it contains implausible things. It talks about a king whose reign was 10000 years!

The Mythical Creation According to Islam (claim by Islam)

Islam is a strictly monotheistic religion. It believes in a God called Allah, which has created everything that exists. The word of God, according to Islam, is the Koran. The Koran talks about the evolution of our universe and how Allah created this synchronized universe.

If we go by modern cosmology, our universe is roughly 13.8 billion years old! That's a lot of time for us. But, the Quran (assuming it to be the word of God) contradicts it by saying that Allah created the universe in 6 days! The following verse claims this-

"We created the heavens and the earth and all between them in Six days, nor did any sense of weariness touch us."- Koran 50:38

In defense of this, Muslims point out that the day mentioned here is not 24 hours but 50,000 earth days, as it is mentioned in verse 70:4-

"The angels and the spirit ascend unto him in a Day the measure whereof is (as) fifty thousand years;"- Koran 70:4

Even if we take this into account, still does not match with our present knowledge of cosmology as 50000* 6 = 300000 years (We are talking about billions of years here.)

Allah didn't even know age of the universe. This suggests that the Koran can't be the word of the creator. Another bogus claim by Allah is the following-

"We created man from sounding clay, from mud moulded into shape;"- Koran 15:26

Did the created create the man from mud? No, it's hilarious to believe this. The Koran was written by people who were living in the 7th century. They were tribal people who didn't have the basic knowledge of science.

It's time for everyone to reevaluate their beliefs and find out the scientific errors. Human society should keep evolving with time, and the time has come to remove the trash of religion. Myths are always myths, and for that matter, religions are always hoaxes.

CHAPTER TWELVE

Why the Red Terror is not the solution: an accusation of fanaticism

"The whole problem with the world is that fools and fanatics are always so certain of themselves, and wiser people so full of doubts."- Bertrand Russell

Fanaticism is the most disturbing state of the human mind. Rationalists and conservatives are always in a tussle with each other. Conservatives want people to follow what's written in scripture. On the contrary, rationalists desire people to expand their worldview and acknowledge enlightening ideas.

We have seen religious fanaticism and bigotry. ISIS, Boko Haram, the Army of God (a Christian terror group), etc are all very dangerous and commit hideous violence. But, we have to acknowledge the other side of the coin. The other side of the coin reveals the atrocities of the so-called "Militant Atheists" that devastated much of Russia and China. People like Stalin or Moa are the names on every religious person's tongue when they debate an atheist.

The critics of the four horsemen (Christopher Hitchens, Richard Dawkins, Sam Harris, and Daniel Dennett) who initiated the atheist revolution did tag them as "radicals" or even "fundamentalists" just on the opposite side of religious fundamentalists. This criticism is very absurd. Neither of them advocated the annihilation of religion by coercive means but believed in secular values.

Now coming back to Militant Atheists, we have to make a differentiation between two sects of atheism. Atheism, by definition, is just a lack of belief in the divine. But if it becomes a political tool, this could lead to militancy or totalitarianism. I want to point out that all rationalist atheists (including me) are secular. On the contrary, the Communists are the ones that are militant or fanatic.

The ideology of Communism was a work by philosopher Karl Max. He was an anti-theist and called religion "the opium of the masses."The two main enemies of Communism are the Bourgeois or the aristocrats and the priests of religious places.

The above image depicts the hierarchy of capitalism purported by Communism

The Russian revolution saw a Communist regime overtaking a monarchy (more precisely, a provisional democratic government that was formed after the fall of Zsars). The chief architect of the Russian revolution of 1917 was Vladimir Lenin. He was a revolutionary, hated the bourgeois and the priests, and made the whole country an authoritarian state. Lenin was an ardent atheist, and in his words he said, "Religion is kind of spiritual gin in which the slaves of capital drown their human shape and claims to a decent life!"

Persecution of Christians and demolishing churches were a part of the Anti-Religious campaign led by the regime of the USSR. Joseph Stalin, the successor of Lenin, was even more anti-religious and wiped out religion from the state. Pamphlets were circulated to demonize religious people as scum or vermin. Some sources reveal that nearly 12 to 20 million Christians became the victims of the Soviet Union, and at least 106,300 clergymen were persecuted between 1937 and 1941.

An example of an anti-religious pamphlet circulated during the Soviet Union's anti-religious campaign

The same case happened with China. The Chinese Communist Party, led by Mao Zedong, seized control over China and turned the whole country into a Socialist state (same as Russia). The Revolution brought a new hostility against religion and the promotion of scientific atheism. The situation became so intense that even holding religious books became a crime! When the CCP annexed Tibet, persecution of Buddhist monks and nuns ravaged the region. This forced the current Dalai Lama to seek refuge in India.

The recent maltreatment of Uighur Muslims in China is another pressing abuse of human rights and should be condemned at all costs. The Uighurs are a Turkic-ethnic group that originates from Central Asia and East Asia. Most of them are practicing Muslims, and China reckons them as terrorists or a threat to national security. And for that matter, has set up training camps to forcefully teach them that their religion is wrong.

Mao Zedong, Stalin, and Lenin, these people were atheists, for sure. But they did not believe in the spirit of democracy and secularism. They suppressed the freedom of religion and weaponized atheism against the believers. This type of fringe-atheism doesn't represent the rational atheists out there (including me). Atheism can lead to totalitarianism. But it does not imply that its basic philosophy is flawed. So, I want to plea to all my fellow believers that stop using the old argument of atheism as another form of extremism. Religions, conversely, induce people to do immoral stuff, and the problem here is not with the people but with the teachings of these religions. A conservative atheist doesn't get his immorality from atheism but a fundamentalist theist does indeed get it from its religious scripture.

Conclusion: The Era Of Skepticism

Someone has rightly said that "the 21st century will be the graveyard century of all organized religions." I don't know who said it, but his or her's prophecy is coming out to be true. The number of unbelievers is increasing day by day, and they are continuously posing a strong challenge against the mighty organized religions (Although, hogus-bogus spiritualism is still another layer of faith that humanity has to overcome).

The total implosion of the Abrahamic religions has hugely sparked the flame of rationality and reason. People are now realizing that faith alone is blind, illogical, and inhumane. This era might turn out to be an era of rationality and atheism, and may the truth prevails.

I want to conclude my book with 50 questions for a theist (sort- of a challenge) -

1) How many Gods are there, and how can you be so sure of the number of gods you believe in? For the Muslims, Christians, and Jews, how do you know that only one God exists? Why not a congregation of Gods or two Gods having fun with each other?

2) Why did he create the universe so inhospitable for life? There are innumerable planets out there in the universe, but only a few can sustain life. Why is it that so?

3) Why did he take so much time to create the sun, then the earth, and then humans? What's the Godly- logic behind this?

4) Why didn't he give us the evidence to conduce us for believing in him?

5) Why does he allow earthquakes, famines, diseases, or landslides? Give me a theodicy that is irrefutable by

atheists.

6) Why did God give vestigial organs to animals and humans?

7) If God knows everything, even the future, why should we pray to him?

8) Why the books of God so ambiguous?

9) What's the need for God to create such a vast universe just for inhabiting a single planet?

10) Why can't he reveal himself in front of all of us right now?